1?

Natural  Disasters

Volcano!

KN DEC 08

For my grandchildren—M. D. B.

To Paul and Anna—J. G. W.

ALADDIN PAPERBACKS
An imprint of Simon & Schuster Children's Publishing Division
1230 Avenue of the Americas, New York, NY 10020
Text copyright © 2008 by Marion Dane Bauer
Illustrations copyright © 2008 by John Wallace
Designed by Christopher Grassi
The text of this book was set in Century Oldstyle BT.
Manufactured in the United States of America
First Aladdin Paperbacks edition September 2008
2 4 6 8 10 9 7 5 3 1
Library of Congress Cataloging-in-Publication Data
Bauer, Marion Dane.
Volcano! / by Marion Dane Bauer ; illustrated by John Wallace.
p.   cm. — (Natural disasters)
1. Volcanoes—Juvenile literature. I. Title.
QE521.3.B39 2008
551.21—dc22
2007046410
ISBN-13: 978-1-4169-2549-1
ISBN-10: 1-4169-2549-X

Natural ⚡ Disasters

Volcano!

By **Marion Dane Bauer**

Illustrated by **John Wallace**

Ready-to-Read
ALADDIN
New York London Toronto Sydney

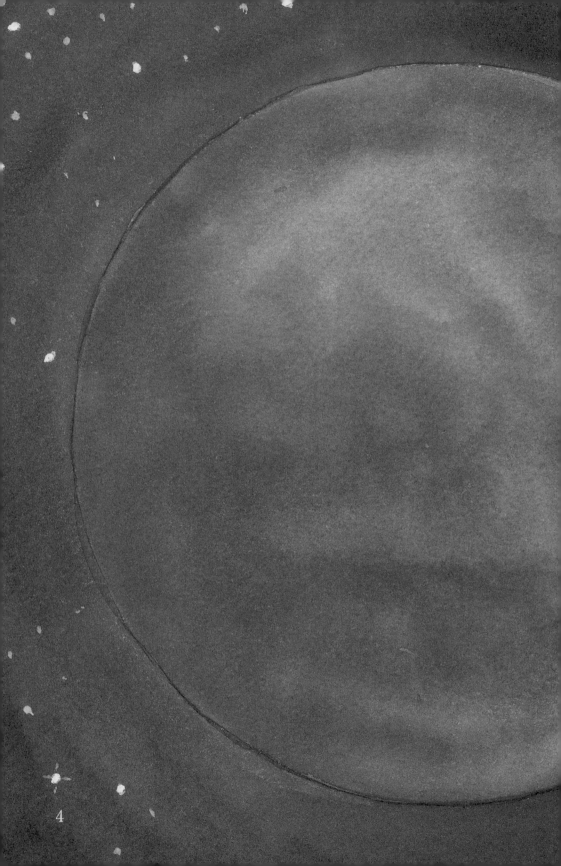

Once our entire Earth
was made of hot gases.

The gases cooled
into hot rock.

A thin crust formed
over the rock.

Volcanoes spewed
melted rock and steam
from inside the Earth.

The steam formed clouds,
then fell back to Earth as rain.

The rain made oceans,
rivers, and lakes.

The world we know was born
because of volcanoes!

Today, volcanoes still
shape our world.

Beneath Earth's hard, cool crust,
the rock is hot and
mixed with gases.

This rock is magma.

Magma

Hot magma is lighter
than the cool rock above,
so it pushes up and up.

It gathers in magma chambers.
The magma builds and builds
until it finds a crack or a hole.
Then it escapes onto the crust.

Volcano!

Some volcanoes are red.
They spit out red-hot,
melted rock called lava.

Some volcanoes are gray.

They spit out rock and ash.

Lava forms mountains

and islands and plains.

Ash makes the soil rich
so plants can grow.

But watch out!
When a volcano erupts,
get out of the way!

We are too small
and too easily broken
to stay close by

while our Earth
is being made new.

Interesting Facts about Volcanoes

⚡ The word *volcano* comes from the name of the Roman god of fire, Vulcan.

⚡ The newest land to be formed by a volcano is an island off the coast of Iceland called Surtsey. It appeared in 1963. Surtsey means "Surtur's island." Surtur was a fire giant in Norse mythology.

⚡ Volcanic activity is forming a new island in Hawaii too. The island already has a name, Loihi, but it will not rise above the ocean for another 10,000 years.

⚡ Scientists who study volcanoes are called *volcanologists*. Sometimes volcanologists wear protective clothing and climb down into the mouths of volcanoes.

⚡ Most volcanic eruptions occur at the bottom of the ocean, but no scientist has ever seen an eruption under the ocean. They see the effects afterward. The pressure of the water keeps under-ocean volcanoes from being violent.

⚡ California has at least sixty-six volcanoes. Alaska has some of the most violent volcanoes on Earth. Hawaii has volcanoes that erupt all the time.

⚡ When Mount St. Helens in Washington State erupted in 1980, eight billion tons of rock slid down the mountain's side.

⚡ Five-hundred-million people live within five miles of one of the Earth's 1,500 active volcanoes.